# YOUR DEFAULT SETTINGS

ADJUST YOUR AUTOPILOT TO BUILD A MORE STABLE AND IMPACTFUL LIFE

RAD WENDZICH

Cover design by Andrea Stan
Illustrated by Ana Popovic
Creative direction by Rad Wendzich

ISBN 978-1-7342137-0-6

# Dedication

Dear Everly and Hazel,
If I succeed at raising you,
your default settings will be carefully chosen
and unapologetically different than mine.

# Contents

# Introduction

# The Incident

I almost died when I was in my twenties. I was sitting in my living room reading the news. Then, suddenly, I couldn't concentrate on the headlines in front of me. I turned to my pregnant wife and said, "I caannn't easseell." Surprised at what came out of my mouth, I took a few deep breaths and kept trying to correct myself. It didn't work. I wanted to say "I can't read, something is wrong," but all that came out of my mouth was a jumble of words. My wife rushed me to the ER, where I was immediately given a room and asked if I had a will.

Twenty-six tests later, the doctors determined that I had meningoencephalitis, an infection of the brain and spinal cord. Left untreated, bacterial meningoencephalitis has a near 100% mortality rate, and even after treatment, survivors can suffer brain damage, paralysis, or stroke. I was in the lucky pool of survivors with meningoencephalitis caused by a virus rather than bacteria. And, fortunately, I suffered no long-term complications.

The doctors never found the source of the infection, and I was discharged home three days later. I had swollen veins in both of my arms from gallons of fluids, antivirals, and antibiotics that had been pumped into my body. I was 28 years old and in great health before the incident. But for those three days in the hospital, I thought that my time on Earth was coming to an end very soon.

Rarely do we think that our time is finite but near-death experiences can be a useful reminder.

## Death Gives You Focus and Impatience

The reminder that you have limited time in this life can give you focus when you need it most. I use my mortality as a tool to get off my butt. In fact, any time I feel like procrastinating, I remind myself of a line in a Guy Lombardo song: "It's later than you think."

Knowing that time is limited can also make you more impatient to get what you want out of life. It's easier to take action when you start asking questions like *How can I become successful* ***faster****? How can I create the impact I want to have on the world* ***sooner****?*

> It's later than you think.
>
> - GUY LOMBARDO

Death is a great motivator, but motivation is just the beginning. I wrote this book to give you a framework that will be both a shortcut and a strong foundation on your journey toward achieving your life goals.

## You Need a Shortcut

Quality and shortcuts don't always mix, but there are ways that you can be efficient in life without sacrificing quality. For example, I finished high school and college in six years (two years early), graduating from Arizona State University with the highest Summa Cum Laude honors and the Undergraduate Student of the Year award.

A shortcut may not always mean less time in the short term, but rather fewer detours, roundabouts, and do-overs in the long run. A shortcut can serve as a strong foundation that won't need tearing down in a few years. So, the core question is: *How do I achieve my goals not only in the most efficient way but also in a way that lasts?*

## You Don't Need Any More Tactics or Principles

Much of the life advice in self-improvement books covers "tactics" (advice whose practicality varies depending on how similar you are to the advice-giver, such as "keep a journal" or "take a cold shower in the morning") and "principles" (decision-making criteria such as "optimize for the long term" or "treat others how you'd like to be treated").

Both tactics and principles have a place in our lives, but there's also a third aspect that relates to what we do *before* we try a new tactic or principle. This third aspect, our default settings, is the topic of this book. Our defaults are vital because they steer many of our daily decisions. They are often invisible to us and they are very hard to break away from.

## Anybody Can Change

Before we jump in, it's worth noting that following the advice in this book will require you to change. I know all about changing: when I was in high school, I was voted "The Most Shy Guy" among 2,400 students. My peers were right. I never spoke up in class, I was quiet,

I would blush when a stranger spoke to me, and I never volunteered to do anything public. But then I decided to change that.

Four years later, I gave my first prime-time news interview. In my second job out of college, I signed up to give monthly presentations to new employees, including speaking at company-wide conferences in front of 300 people. The point is, no matter what label people may have applied to you in the past, you can change it. Anybody can transform their life as long as they have the right framework to build on.

So, let's get started.

# 1

# Understanding Default Settings

# What Is a Default Setting?

All technology has default settings. Your smartphone has a default internet browser, your refrigerator has a default cooling setting, and your vacuum has a default brush. It's a configuration for the product chosen by the manufacturer. Many of us don't change the defaults on our tech, so they stay that way for a long time. We usually don't know that we *can* change them, or we think the current setting is good enough to do its job.

How do defaults apply to human behavior? Your default settings are your repeated behaviors and beliefs. When you do something by default, you do it without even thinking about it, as if you were on autopilot.

There are a few ways to identify a default setting in your life:

- You can identify defaults in anything you do as second nature that you haven't changed in years. Consider the way you brush your teeth every day, the way you tie your shoes, or the way you put your hands on a steering wheel. What are your patterns of actions, words, and thoughts that have become ingrained over the years?
- You can identify your default settings by looking at your environment. Your defaults aren't necessarily unique to you; others might share the same behaviors. You may jaywalk at a certain traffic light because *everyone* jaywalks at that light, or bring a reusable bag when you go shopping after seeing your neighbors with theirs in the checkout line. Which of your behaviors or beliefs have been shaped by your current or previous communities?
- You can also discover your defaults by comparing yourself to people you've met recently. Perhaps your default setting is putting dishes in a dishwasher differently than your roommates or holding the door

open for other people when others just keep walking. What things do you do differently than other people?

When you answer these questions, you'll realize that you have default settings in all areas of your life.

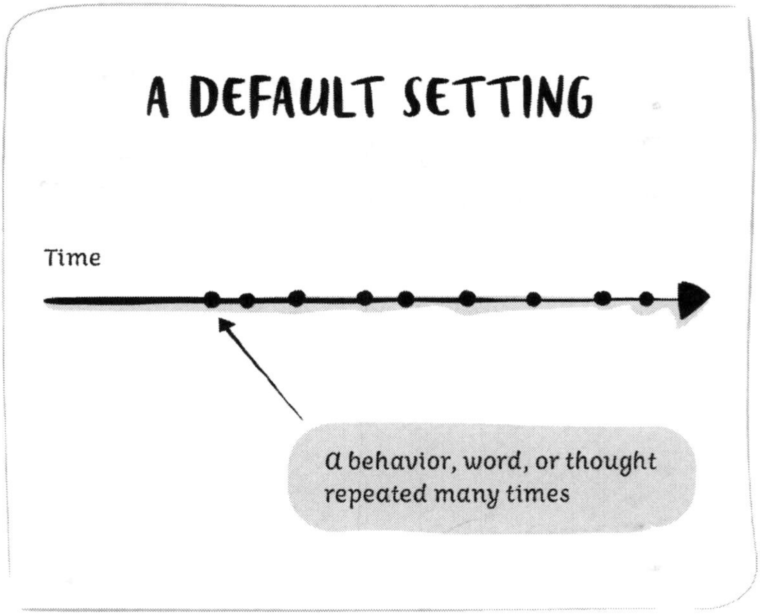

# Why Do We Have Defaults?

Default settings make us more efficient. In computer programs, default settings ensure that new users get value right away when using a product for the first time. When you open a new Word document, the default font type and size are already set and you can start typing right away. An out-of-the-box smartphone comes with a default camera app on its home screen—you don't have to research or download anything to start taking photos. In short, defaults save us time and save us from making hard decisions when we have limited experience. And just like in technology, the default settings in your life can be incredibly useful.

A default way of greeting people means you don't have to scramble for words every time you see somebody. A default method of folding laundry makes it faster to put your clean clothes away. A default route to work means you'll arrive on time without getting lost.

When a repeated action becomes second nature, you can finish it without even having to think about it. For example, during a typical commute to work, you don't need to devote brainpower to remembering where to turn or where to merge; you essentially function on autopilot. A default commute frees up your mental capacity to solve other problems, like planning your tasks for the day or brainstorming ways to contribute to a new project.

# How Did We Get Our Defaults?

You aren't born with your default settings—they are conditioned into you.

Your first defaults were set by your parents. When you were little, your parents looked after you and ensured that all of your needs were met so you could explore and grow. As a kid, you had no important life decisions to make: all decisions—where you lived, where you went to school, where you traveled for vacations, where you got your hair cut, where you deposited your first savings—were narrowed to a few choices or made for you entirely. This supervision is helpful when you don't know much, and these defaults set the foundation for your own decision-making as you get older and learn more.

Your parents play a key role in shaping you as a person. As you become more and more independent and go out into the world on your own, your neighbors, teachers, peers, and people you meet online—rather than just your parents—start to determine what kind of human you're becoming and what defaults you adopt.

There's a concept in psychology called *group identity*, which states that the group you identify with influences your personal goals and actions. The similarities and common interests within a group create stronger bonds and make it easier for members to relate to each other. Think back to when you were a kid. Chances are that the sports you tried, video games you played, or TV shows you watched were also popular within your circle of friends. You didn't invent your free-time activities. Your interests likely originated from your community's interests. You saw something in person, on TV, or online, and then you tried it yourself.

# YOUR PARENT'S DECISIONS

Hometown

Bank

Religion

Diet

...

# YOUR DECISIONS

(AS A TEENAGER)

☑ Same as parent

☐ Custom

Settings last updated: **Never**

Your surroundings also influence your ideas. If I asked you to think of any country in the world, you'd more than likely name a country you've either been to, heard of, or read about in the past. Even when we use our imagination to create something we perceive as "new," it's really just a mash-up of things we've previously experienced or heard of. The sources of your ideas are limited to your encounters up until this point.

The way you sound originates from your community, too. Your accent might not stay exactly the same if you move around, but no matter what you sound like, your speech patterns will always be influenced by your experiences and the places you've lived. For example, there are more than twenty dialects of English in the United States. Each has its own word choices, sentence structuring, and intonations that are picked up through exposure. The patterns that surround you become your default simply because it's what everyone around you sounds like.

You may not be aware of all the things you absorb from those around you, but community, and the time you spend *in* a community, shapes your ideas, your interests, and your voice.

# Community Voices Become Your Decisions

Your community influences more than just your ideas and interests. The conversations that take place around you, even if you aren't really listening, can influence your future decisions too. When I was growing up, my parents would gossip about our neighbors after work: "So-and-so got a well-paying engineering job." "Mr. X got an impressive promotion and raise." These weren't conversations I was particularly interested in at the time, but my brain stored the idea that an engineering job was impressive and could make a lot of money. So when I turned eighteen and needed to make my first career decision, what field did I choose? Electrical engineering. It took some reflection to realize that I didn't actually enjoy engineering, but had only chosen it because of the ingrained belief that it would be lucrative and make me respected and successful—all because of a few conversations overheard during my childhood.

And conversations are just the beginning. Some of your standards of behavior come from observing how people in your community act as much as what they say. You probably greet a cashier the same way as the people before you. You may sort your recycling, garbage, and compost because your community expects it, or you might litter because it's commonplace and your parents, teachers, and neighbors don't care.

The influence on your decisions isn't even limited to your physical community. When you started using social media, you probably posted whatever you found interesting, but after a while, you may have adjusted your content based on what got the most likes. I've certainly taken down some of my posts after not getting very many likes. I speculated about why I couldn't get more traction: if my friends didn't like my update, they may be thinking I'm too boring, too self-centered, or not entertaining enough. It's human nature to desire inclusion and acceptance and the fastest way to this goal is maintaining the status quo. Don't ruffle too many feathers and you can be safe as part of the flock. Negative feedback and silence are hard to receive, while the feeling of belonging is easy and satisfying to accept.

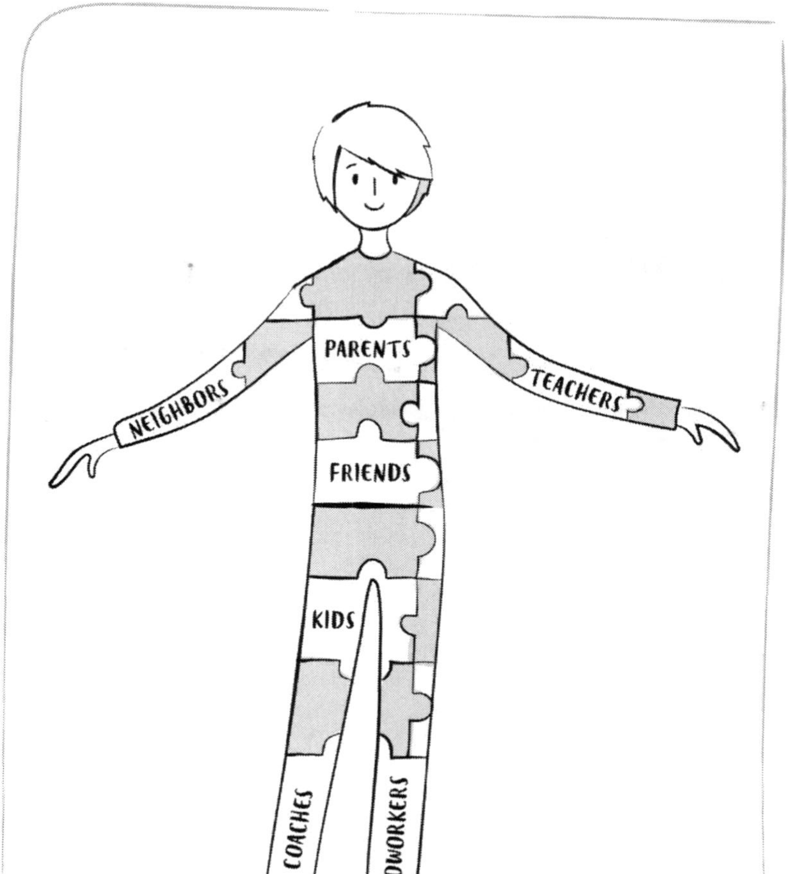
PARENTS
NEIGHBORS
TEACHERS
FRIENDS
KIDS
COACHES
COWORKERS

# Why Change a Default Setting?

When we're young, default settings help us fit in. But these same default settings can be a problem later if they persist without reevaluation. Unexamined defaults can end up taking our life in the wrong direction.

Although default settings in technology are designed to create the best experience for the majority of consumers, there still isn't a "one size fits all" answer. Your smartphone's pre-installed internet browser app may be slower and less secure than another option. Your refrigerator's default thermostat settings may require recalibration to keep your food from spoiling in a warmer environment. Your vacuum's default brush may be perfect for carpet, but not as efficient if you have tile floors.

In general, default settings can be problematic for three reasons:

## #1 Defaults Become Outdated

Default settings—both in software and in our lives—are most helpful when we wouldn't know where to begin otherwise. But that ignorance is temporary. We'll always have default settings—shortcuts for making decisions, patterns of behaviors, and habits—but we don't need to hold on to our *original* settings over time. When we have limited time, we don't want to waste it on things that don't move our goals forward. "Greatness," as American historian James Harvey Robinson said, is "courage in escaping from old ideas and old standards."

## #2 Defaults Are Impersonal

Our default settings are like hand-me-down clothes. When we get them, we don't have a choice of size, style, or color, and they usually don't fit us as well as they fit their previous owner. Because your default settings are initially set by your parents and community, they're impersonal and set without any consideration for your individuality.

Defaults within communities are optimized for the average, not for any one person. "To be yourself in a world that is constantly trying to make you something else," Ralph Waldo Emerson argued, "is the greatest accomplishment." While I love my parents, grandparents, and the community I grew up in, I'm more than just the sum of those influences.

## #3 Defaults Are Limiting

Accepting the default settings created by others (even people we trust, like our parents, teachers, and friends) means that we're also accepting their assumptions, which are likely going to limit our individual growth and impact.

An expert in growth, Elon Musk, has a mantra to approach problem-solving by looking at "first principles." This means ignoring the conclusions that others have made, starting with fundamental basics that you know are true and building up from there. Revising assumptions ensures that nothing is missed. But to do so, you have to evaluate your routine behaviors and be willing to change any that aren't working.

You will make progress with your original defaults, but not as fast as if you examine and change them.

# The Key Benefit of Changing Your Defaults

The most critical moment of your life happens when you decide to examine *and adjust* your default settings.

Your awareness of your default settings, your ability to evaluate them, and your willingness to change them are the key components of correcting your course in life. There will be several benefits along the way:

- While your old defaults may have been holding you back, your new settings can help you upgrade all parts of your life, making it even more positive, more energized, and more stable.
- Adjusting your defaults means you are more in control of your life. Each adjustment you make is a purposeful change in the direction your life is taking and in defining success on your own terms.

- The journey of defining new habits and beliefs will make you dig deep and examine what you truly enjoy and hate. The more you know about yourself, the more aligned your future decisions will be to your goals.
- Updating your routine can also help you get ahead. Most people don't change their defaults. When you do, you will stand out more from your peers.
- And because default settings drive recurring behaviors, the effects of changing them will become a lasting foundation. Once changed, these behaviors will become your new autopilot.

The main benefit of updating your default settings, however, is **your long-term impact**.

Humans have an inherent desire to leave a lasting legacy. Everything we do contributes to how we will be remembered, but having a significant impact is not easy. In fact, more often than not, our impact is suppressed. We end up in jobs that don't leverage our strengths.

Our interpersonal interactions are polite, but essentially transactional and shallow. Our digital habits consume a lot of our time, leaving us feeling too drained to create something new.

To have the most positive impact on others, we need to align our work to our strengths and passions, spread love in our interactions, and hand-pick our digital content to recharge us. We can't accomplish these things without first analyzing our defaults. Updating and personalizing your default settings means that your autopilot will take you—and your impact—further.

In the following chapters, we'll use this lens of long-term impact to approach analyzing and changing our defaults.

**MAKE FASTER PROGRESS: SHARE AND DISCUSS YOUR DEFAULT SETTINGS WITH OTHERS**

Go to yourdefaultsettings.com/community or use a hashtag #yourdefaultsettings

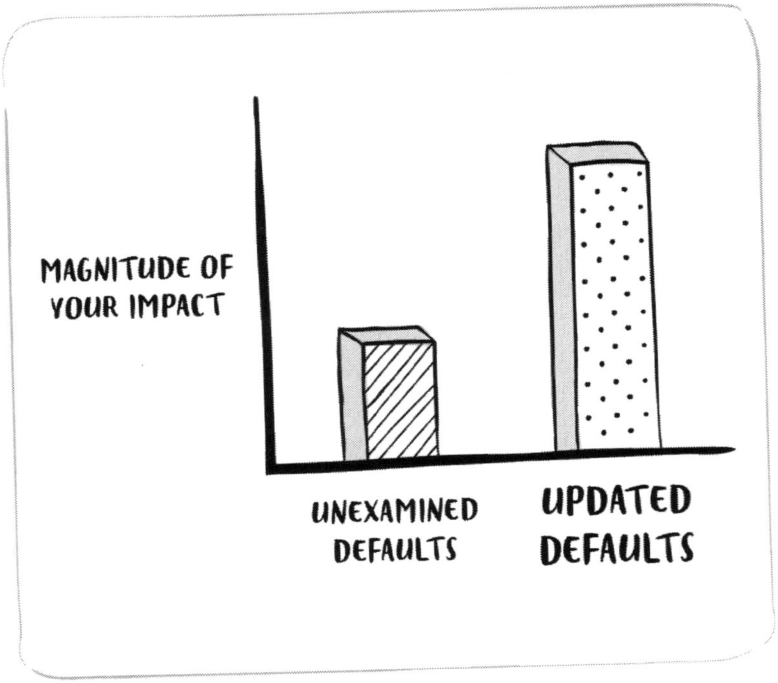
MAGNITUDE OF YOUR IMPACT
UNEXAMINED DEFAULTS
UPDATED DEFAULTS

## Chapter Summary

- Your default settings are the patterns of actions, words, and thoughts that have become ingrained in you over the years. Many times, you don't even notice or think about them, as if you were on autopilot.
- Default settings allow us to be more efficient, to make better decisions, and to build strong communities.
- You aren't born with your default settings—they are conditioned into you by your parents, communities, and the content you pay attention to, both in person and online.
- Your original default settings may not be the right ones for you—in fact, they are probably outdated and impersonal. You are unique and your defaults should be unique to you.
- When you aren't held back by your original default settings, you have a higher likelihood of success and greater impact.

# 2

# Changing Default Settings

# The 3-step Formula

Let's say we want to teach a ten-year-old to play an instrument. She doesn't know where to start, or even which instrument to play. How could we help her?

First, she should get some exposure to different options. This could mean watching videos of various instruments, bands, and music styles; visiting a music store; or attending a live performance. Then she should reflect on which instrument she liked the most. Finally, she needs to commit to learning. This could mean buying her own instrument, signing up for a class, and setting a schedule to practice consistently.

As with learning an instrument—or anything else that's brand-new to us—changing a default setting involves three steps: new exposures, reflection, and commitment to change. Let's talk more about each one of these steps.

# Step 1: Seek New Exposures

> *People never improve unless they look to some standard or example higher and better than themselves.*
>
> - TYRON EDWARDS

As mentioned in the first chapter, our ideas are limited by what we've encountered in the past. We can only create new connections between things that are already stored in our brains. The same applies to our settings. We can't change our beliefs or habits to a different course of action if we don't know our options.

To change a default setting, then, you must first realize that there's another way. You can learn about other options by becoming exposed to new people and their

# OPTIONS ARE OFTEN HIDDEN FROM YOUR INITIAL VIEW

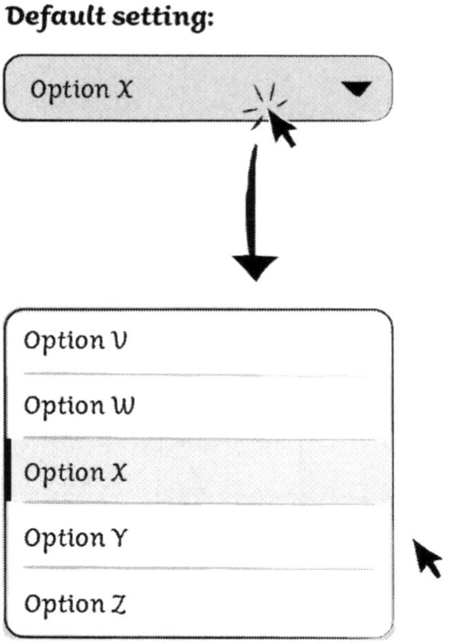

ideas, and to do that, you have to leave the comfort zone of your current environment.

How long you spend outside of your comfort zone could be short or long. It could mean taking a trip to a new country, signing up for a summer workshop, or even just changing up where you eat lunch for a month. That being said, the more immersed you are, and the starker the contrast between your new experience and your typical default settings, the more effective this exercise will be. Traveling to an all-inclusive resort surrounded by staff catering to you may be relaxing, but it won't change your life. Seek not just novelty, but also a bit of discomfort.

If you're impatient for change, make the departure from your norm more permanent. Move to a different school, job, neighborhood, or city, and you'll force a faster and more complete immersion. There was a key moment in my life when I went from being a C student to an A+ student. My grades changed overnight and never dropped below an A again. That big change? Moving from Europe to the United States. The permanent move resulted in my complete immersion in a new culture, with a new climate, language, and people, and it was a shock to the previous habits I had established. I wanted to build stability and a good reputation in my new environment, which motivated me to care more about my school grades.

New exposures can also come from digital content. Nowadays, there are millions of communities on the internet that you can join without getting up from your chair. You can change what you watch with a few clicks. You can listen to new audiobooks or podcasts on your commute. If you don't know where to start, an easy first step is browsing digital content by category and choosing something new that looks thought-provoking. You could jump into art, comedy, health, or technology and listen to an episode or chapter of a podcast or book to see the topics and language used by a different community.

Next, move from *observing* to *doing*. Experiencing something new isn't just about *seeing* new things, it's

NEW COMMUNITY
OLD COMMUNITY

about *trying* new things. Think of it like a visit to an ice cream shop: if you're going to change up your go-to choice, you have to taste a sample of new flavors to see if you'll like them, not just look at them in the case. Interested in playing guitar? Pick one up! Think you have untapped artistic talent? Start creating! Curious whether video blogging is something you'll enjoy? Record a few videos!

Once you've tried some new things, it's time to evaluate all the experiences you've collected and decide where you should settle.

# Step 2: Reflect

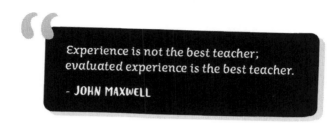

> Experience is not the best teacher; evaluated experience is the best teacher.
>
> - JOHN MAXWELL

I believe in shortcuts to success, and regular reflection is one of them.

To reflect appropriately, you need to pause, step away from your daily routine, and take stock of how you feel about your recent experiences.

Writing things down can help, but you can also reflect while sharing your experiences with a friend. Reflecting after a few experiences may make it easier to notice themes, but you can also reflect after a single event. Going somewhere new can make it easier to break your routine and focus on reflection, but you can also reflect during your regular commute.

Reflection is flexible and unique to each person but there are two strategies that I found most helpful in my sessions. First, look at both the positives and negatives. Knowing what bothers you makes it easier to avoid it in the future (or to turn that feeling from a frustration to a solution). And once you know what you really want, you can work that much faster to achieve it. Second, keep a long-term perspective when reflecting. Exercising isn't pleasant in the moment. Starting a new diet is laborious at the beginning. Being assigned entry-level tasks may not be enjoyable. But when you think of them as stepping stones to where you want to be in five years or as necessary sacrifices to helping you make a difference in the world, you'll realize they are worth your time even if they're not immediately gratifying.

You may still be able to find your way to what you want without reflection, but you run the risk of committing yourself to a path that is adjacent to the one you should be following, and ultimately having to backtrack to get on the right path.

The goal of this activity is to learn about your preferences as quickly as possible and immediately apply what you have uncovered to future decision-making.

Experience
Experience
Experience
ALWAYS MOVING FORWARD
Experience
Experience
Experience
– +
PAUSING TO REFLECT

# Step 3: Commit

To truly change something in your life, you have to commit yourself to the change fully, which means you have to commit to it over and over again. This is true whether the commitment is big or small. During wedding vows, people promise to love and care for each other for the rest of their lives for better or for worse. This isn't just a vague happily ever after; it's a daily commitment to love and care for their partner, even when it is difficult. True commitment requires consistency over time.

Because default settings are created after years of influence by your current community, changing those default settings means having more contact with "the new" than "the old". You can do this by increasing exposure to what you want—start spending more time with the guitar if you want to play better, subscribe to an instructional video channel to improve your skills, sit next to the people you admire to learn from them.

Alternatively, you can distance yourself from what you want to avoid—hide the gaming console, leave your job to pursue a stronger passion, or stop answering your toxic friend's text messages.

Real commitment involves changing how and where you spend your time. If you haven't been repeating the new behavior, haven't joined a new community, or haven't moved, you haven't truly committed.

Commitment to a new setting is hard but it also means expanding your horizons. It means visiting new places, embarking on new adventures, making new friends, and creating new memories. You may have already seen it firsthand if you've made changes to your environment in the past. For example, if you switched majors in college, changed careers, left home, or spent a year abroad, you probably felt energized and liberated. A change to your surroundings will likely improve how you feel and how you think. And in the long term, the reward for this commitment is a new default setting.

# TEST OF COMMITMENT: CONSISTENCY

| M | T | W | TH | F | SA | SU |
|---|---|---|---|---|---|---|
| | action | | | | | |
| | | | | | | |
| | | | | | | |
| | | | | | | |
| | | | | | | |

NOT COMMITTED

VS

| M | T | W | TH | F | SA | SU |
|---|---|---|---|---|---|---|
| | action | | | | | |
| | action | | | | | |
| | action | | | | | |
| | action | | | | | |
| | action | | | | | |

COMMITTED

# Which Default Settings Should You Examine First?

Now that you know how to change a default setting—seek new exposures, reflect, and commit—the next question becomes: which defaults should you evaluate first?

If your goal is stability and impact, there are three critical default settings that are quietly steering many of your decisions and determining the path you take in life. These settings affect the areas where you spend most of your waking hours: at work, at home, and in interactions with other people everywhere in-between.

In the next chapters, we'll examine your default settings across these three areas and walk through how to find the right settings for you.

## Chapter Summary

- It takes three steps to change any default setting: seek new exposures, reflect, and commit.
- You can't change a default setting without changing your influences. You must immerse yourself in another community or try new things. Leave your hometown, change the places where you eat or play, or join a new community online.
- Reflection is a shortcut to success. It will help you learn about yourself faster and enable you to use what you've learned in your future decisions.
- Real commitment requires repetition of a new behavior until it becomes a new default.

# 3

# Personal Life Settings

# Leisure Time Autopilot

Every day around the world, people count down the hours until their work duties are over and their personal time can begin.

We love our personal time. It's more fun than work because it's unstructured, spontaneous, and deadline-free. But if you look a little closer, you'll realize that the evenings and weekends that make up personal time are time spent on autopilot. Three things—community trends, geographic location, and digital algorithms—likely limit how you've been spending your free time:

- **Community trends:** Rollerblading took the nation by storm in the '90s. Velour tracksuits were the loungewear of choice in the early 2000s. Fortnite is currently the most popular video game in the world. We tend to do what others around us are doing, and it is important to realize how much community trends affect our personal choice of recreational activities.

- **Geographic location:** The physical environment around you limits what you can do on a regular basis. Your closest friends are most likely people who live nearby. Your activities are dictated by what the local climate's like and what's available nearby. (For example, it's more difficult to take up skiing if you don't live anywhere near the mountains.)
- **Digital algorithms:** The function of computer-generated algorithms is to keep you engaged as long as possible and eager to come back for more. You will never reach the end of your news feed. You get to the end of a TV show only to see automatic suggestions of what you should watch next. These personalized recommendations have shaped your digital routine—what you read, watch, and listen to every day after work — and kept you on that path for months or even years.

## YOUR STARTING POINT

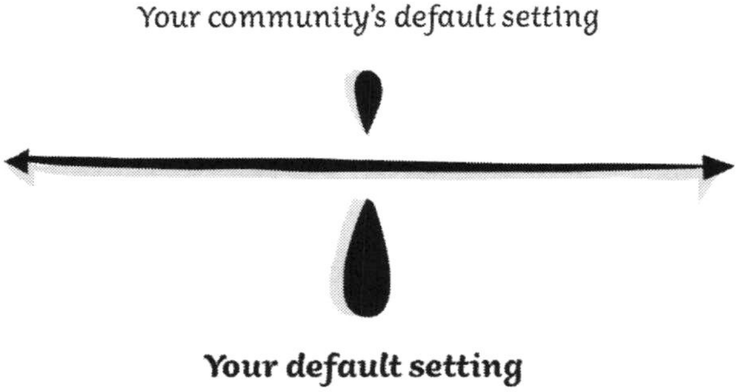


You start out aligned to your community's defaults: with the sports you play, movies you watch, and traditions you adopt.

Because personal time is "free time," you may not think to examine it, but it too is worth a look since there are such strong external influences on the videos you watch, stories you read, and traditions you adopt. You can continue your previous routine, or you can reevaluate your free time activities to make sure they are producing the outcomes you want in your life. Your personal time defaults should have a deliberate role in your life: they should boost your positivity, advance your health and relationships, and promote growth and development. When you go to bed each night, you should feel satisfied that you've invested in areas you care about.

Next, we'll look at the three main areas that make up your personal time: entertainment, friends, and ideologies.

# Choose Positive Entertainment

Media outlets know how to get our attention. They capitalize on our obsession for sensational news, drama-filled reality TV, and dopamine-inducing likes on social media. It's easy to get stuck in the vortex of trending topics, viral videos, and never-ending breaking news. Sometimes, it feels like *all* of the content around us is trying to trick us into paying attention.

A common default is to simply consume the content presented to you. But a better default is to be purposeful about the media you pay attention to. Your default digital content should not only recharge you but also inspire you. Being reenergized can be contagious: A TED talk can spark a deep conversation with a friend, a humorous shared moment can relieve stress for a coworker, a great book can be the calming retreat needed for you to bring enthusiasm to your group project.

Changing your entertainment defaults should incorporate two steps:

1. Find types of content that feel uplifting, educational, or energizing. Since you can realistically consume only a handful of different types of entertainment during your personal time, pick between three and five favorites from the YouTube channels, TV shows, podcasts, newsletters, books, social media channels, or games that have the most positive impact on you.
2. Click the *Subscribe*, *Follow*, or *Download All* button to have your positive content ready when you are.

Once you've intentionally set up your digital content, consider how to maximize its impact. Sometimes, all that's needed to boost your benefit is asking "What can I learn from this?". You can ask this of any type of media, even video games. Gaming may seem like a complete waste of time, but if you approach it with a goal that will matter after you stop playing, it doesn't have to be.

## GOOD WEEKEND

## GREAT WEEKEND

*A great weekend is when you feel not only recharged, but also uplifted, reconnected with your loved ones, and inspired by new ideas.*

I spent a fair amount of my adolescence playing an online video game called *Tibia*. The goal of the game was to work with other players to defeat monsters and trade virtual items. Cooperation was key to success in the game, and English was the primary language spoken by the other players. My first language was Polish, but my desire to be good at the game motivated me to pay close attention to English grammar and learn all the words I didn't understand. Even after I started to get a little bored with the game, I kept playing because I was learning English at a faster rate than I was in school. Hours of playing the game ended up saving me years of formal education. When I moved to the U.S. a couple of years later, I took an English placement test and qualified for an English class for native speakers. In short, the best form of entertainment should always include some form of education.

Most of what we consume by default is high-traffic, low-payoff entertainment. The final step of setting up a new, positive stream of content is to unsubscribe, unfollow, and delete sources of negative content. Do a quick scroll through your social media accounts. If seeing someone's name or photos makes you feel bad about yourself, angry, or negative in any way, unfollow them! You want every log-in to social media to be a source of positive emotions and inspiration.

# Be Picky about Your Friends

We previously talked about how fitting in is part of our human instinct—talking, dressing, and acting like others around us. Since the people you spend time with are the main influence on your default settings, from the way you speak to your health goals and your habit, be picky and purposeful about who those people are. Inevitably, both their good and their bad parts will rub off on you.

By default, our first relationships are a result of our location. We play sports and go to school with people who live in our neighborhood. In college and in the workplace, we tend to associate most with those who sit near us. And because we usually don't have a choice of our work desk or who our neighbors are, the people we see and talk to most often are defined by chance.

# WHICH QUALITIES ARE IMPORTANT TO YOU IN A FRIEND?

- [ ] Available when needed
- [ ] Punctual
- [ ] Present when you're hanging out
- [ ] Good listener
- [ ] Emotionally supportive
- [ ] Good problem solver
- [ ] Inspiring you to grow
- [ ] Funny
- [ ] Adventurous
- [ ] Honest about your growth areas
- [ ] Forgiving
- [ ] ______

Download a printable version of this cheat sheet at yourdefaultsettings.com/book

A French poet, Jacques Delille, said that "Chance makes our parents, but choice makes our friends." To build more intentional relationships, you first have to list the qualities you value most in a friend. Describe the ideal person to have by your side both when you are at your best and when you are in need and don't hold back.

Once you write down the qualities that are important to you, list the three people you spend most of your time with and see how they rank against your quality bar. Remember that one friend likely won't satisfy all your needs. However, if a current friend isn't meeting *any* of your key needs, discuss these shortcomings with them to create an opportunity for growth in your friendship. You can also ask how *you* can be a better friend to *them*. Great friendships are mutually rewarding.

There may also be times when you realize that your current relationships are toxic. When this is the case, it's best to scale back how much time you spend together, as difficult as that may be. Acknowledge the benefits you gained from this relationship, recognize that you have learned what you could, and move on. Drastic and unpleasant breakups are rarely necessary in these cases, you can simply allow bad friendships to fade out while you spend time with a new group.

Because proximity dictates many of our friendships, the easiest way to make new friends is to change your physical location. Sit next to people you admire. Choose jobs based on the quality of people at an organization. Get involved in extracurricular activities or volunteer organizations that involve people you respect. Invite your role models for coffee or lunch. Don't do it once or twice, either; make it your new default until all of your close friends meet or exceed your quality bar.

# Improve or Redefine Your Family

When you come back to your family after upgrading your default settings out in the world, you may notice more differences between you and them than ever before.

The differences may be clashes of default settings. Your parents' habits may start bothering you after you've seen things done in a different way. Your siblings' beliefs may now be the opposite of yours after you've gained a different perspective from your new friends.

A good approach to these differences is curiosity—ask "why?". When we're on autopilot, we often forget how our habits started, but there's always a reason behind a recurring behavior. When you're respectful and curious, you may learn something that isn't visible on the surface. Throwing clothes in drawers rather than hanging them up may save time downstream. The familiar brand of dish soap may have been chosen as the best "green" option. Driving habits may have been shaped by past tickets or accidents.

If you find out that a default setting may be limiting someone in your family, discuss a potential adjustment with them in a non-judgmental way. If a family gathering feels like an obligation, take initiative to make it more meaningful: Create a new activity that helps family members bond in an engaging and positive way. When you learn something new that saves time—a smartphone shortcut, a grocery-delivery service, or a hair-styling routine—you could share its benefits and teach your family how to do it.

Sometimes, differences between your and your family's default settings restrict your growth. If your family has strong opinions or expectations that interfere with your pursuit of success as you define it—maybe they don't agree with your career goals, partner, or lifestyle—it's okay to create some distance. You can appreciate the sacrifices your family has made for you, and you can accept that they have the best intentions for you, but also recognize that you won't be happy living someone else's dream. And when it comes to deciding how to spend your life, your opinion matters more than theirs. A parent's role is to be your consultant, not your boss.

You can evaluate your family with the same scrutiny as you do your friends—if a family member isn't empowering, encouraging, or supportive when you need them, you should limit the time you spend with them. You can even redefine what "family" means to you—family may very well include some of your non-relative friends. Richard Bach summarized it well: "The bond that links your true family is not one of blood, but of respect and joy in each other's life. Rarely do members of one family grow up under the same roof."

# CLOSE FAMILY

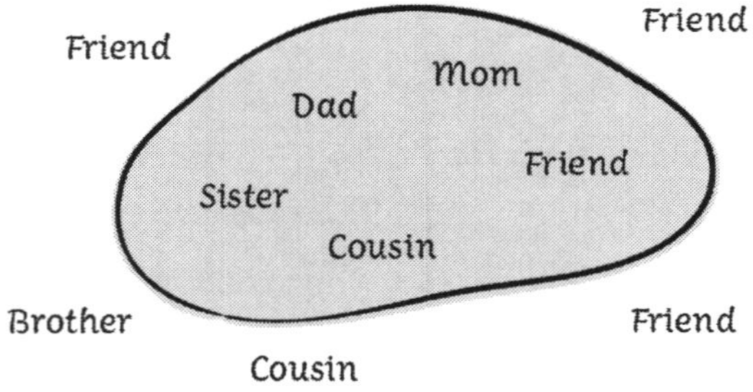


Choose who to include in your closest circle

# Be Skeptical about Your Community's Beliefs

In his book *Sapiens: A Brief History of Humankind*, historian and author Yuval Noah Harari describes how over the course of history, humans developed a special skill that enabled us to cooperate and form communities with strangers, thereby becoming the most successful organisms on Earth: the ability to create and organize ourselves around common beliefs such as religions, political parties, and social movements.

These shared beliefs also influence a lot of activities in our free time—holiday traditions, local events, and family obligations—but because they're so ingrained in our communities, they are rarely talked about.

I like to split these shared beliefs into two types:

- **Widespread ideologies:** Beliefs and behaviors that are built into the structure of our everyday lives, such as our universal agreement to drive on a given side of the road or that there are borders between countries and we need passports to cross them.
- **Limited ideologies:** Beliefs and behaviors that a lot of people—but not everybody—support. They include religious rituals, opinions about other cultures, the American Dream, and Santa Claus. Their influence is confined to countries, cities, and communities.

Some shared ideologies are helpful because they ensure structure and order in our lives. Others (especially the "limited ideologies") may make you spend time on things you don't care about. They can push you to strive for a specific goal but can also make you blind to options that are better for you. Or they may make you fear something you haven't tried, even if there's no real reason to be afraid.

So, how do we change a default belief? As with other default settings, it comes down to the three steps of exposure to new experiences, reflection, and commitment.

For example, my beliefs about success changed when I was seventeen. I picked up a book called *Harmonic Wealth* by James Arthur Ray. Before this, I subscribed to the common belief that "success" basically meant becoming a millionaire. But Ray's definition of success proposed harmony across five areas: financial, relational, mental, physical, and spiritual. That framing resonated with me, and so my pursuit of success became more about developing positive habits in each of these five areas rather than a pursuit of just money. When I write New Year's resolutions, I write a goal for each of the categories. Last year, the list included rebalancing my stock market portfolio, bi-weekly workouts, a better diet, regular meditation, and scheduled dates with my wife. Without coverage across those five areas, I don't consider my list complete. This one book helped me redefine success, which allowed me to reframe my goals.

It can be helpful to think of the limited ideologies as

spectrums where your default setting is one point on the scale. Political views are one example—the scale ranges from conservative to liberal, with most people's opinions falling somewhere in the middle. In everyday life, we amass items with an approach that's somewhere on the spectrum of extravagance (acquiring and collecting possessions) to minimalism (removing or recycling extra stuff). There are also many ways to celebrate holidays, which themselves are a limited ideology. Thanksgiving can be a planned family event with turkey and football, or an event that changes every year, with friends instead of family and no TV playing in the background. You should decide what you want your default to be.

When beliefs are deep-seated within your country, family, or group of friends, it's hard to even notice them. To find out when you should diverge from your community's default, there are four things you can do: (1) Question moments when a tradition feels like an obligation, (2) challenge popular stereotypes, (3) be skeptical of joining long lines and large crowds, and (4) be skeptical of recurring events, especially when you can't describe their benefit. Then identify the opposite end in the spectrum of that ideology and choose a new point that energizes you and feels right for where you want to take your life.

## CHOOSE A POINT ON THE SPECTRUM

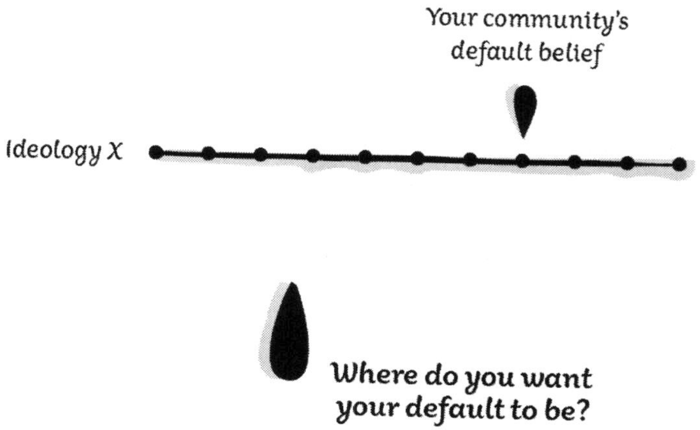

# Start by Cutting Things Out

Our personal time may be unstructured, but it's also full of various activities: people regularly come in and out of our lives, emails impatiently await our response, news stories, viral videos, and device notifications scream for our attention every minute of every day…

We can either react by trying to grab as much of the incoming flow as possible, or we can get into the habit of ignoring parts of it to make room for the new. There are many ways to do the latter:

- Click "cancel," "close," and "not now" more often.
- Uninstall time-sucking apps on your phone.
- Remove the TV from your bedroom (or from your house entirely!).

- Unfollow toxic friends on social media.
- RSVP "no" to invitations that feel like obligations.
- Walk away when you see long lines.
- Make your entertainment duration shorter. If you can't get yourself to stop, set a timer, then do a wildly different activity—push-ups, a walk outside, take a nap, or sing a song. When you stimulate a different part of your brain, it's easier to say no to the previous activity.

Start by cutting the largest time-suckers first. It's difficult to subscribe to new digital content, start hanging out with new people, or begin a new family tradition when your old activities monopolize your attention. Create space for the new by removing the old.

# PERSONAL TIME FILTER

**ACCEPT**

- [ ] Recharging
- [ ] Uplifting
- [ ] Positive
- [ ] Empowering
- [ ] Aligned to your goals
- [ ] ____________________

**REJECT**

Everything else

## Chapter Summary

- Your leisure activities are affected by the people you hang out with and by the places you spend your time in. To change your default activities, change your surroundings (online and offline).
- Subscribe to digital content that not only recharges you but also inspires positive emotions, advances your health, or helps you develop a new skill.
- Define qualities that are important to you in a friendship and spend more time with people who help you grow. Place yourself in environments where you're among people you admire.
- A clash with your family may be a clash of default settings. When this happens, be curious. Create some distance if needed.
- Avoid family traditions and societal beliefs that subtract from your life.

# 4

# Work Settings

# Default Criteria for Accepting a Job

If you couldn't work for your current employer tomorrow, what are the top five things you'd look for in your next job?

Your career is made up of many jobs and projects. Even though the jobs may seem very different on the surface, they are often connected by the *criteria* you used when accepting the positions, such as salary, commute time, your parents' or teachers' suggestions, or alignment with your previous experience. You're unlikely to stay with the same company for a lifetime, but you will stay on the same career path as long as your criteria stay the same.

The best way to evaluate your criteria is to look at your resume. How did you choose to take the first job on your current career path? Your list of reasons will likely include both the tangibles, like insurance or a stable paycheck, and intangibles, like company reputation and learning opportunities.

As with all defaults, when your criteria for accepting a job stay unexamined and unchanged, it affects all future decisions too.

# CHOOSE TOP 5 REASONS YOU'RE AT YOUR CURRENT JOB

- ☐ High salary
- ☐ Builds on my previous experience
- ☐ Good benefits
- ☐ Leverages my strengths
- ☐ Short commute
- ☐ Flexible schedule
- ☐ Aligned to my passion
- ☐ Continues a family tradition
- ☐ Offers learning opportunities
- ☐ High quality co-workers
- ☐ ________

# Your Criteria Should Prioritize "You"

Other than sleep, work takes up the largest chunk of our lives. This means that your choices about where to work—your default criteria for accepting a job—are the most influential decisions when it comes to how you'll spend your life.

The criteria that are in your and your legacy's best interest are internal—they consider your strengths, your passions, and things that are important to you. When somebody looks at your resume, they should easily see what you care about. The wrong criteria are dominated by external influences like others' expectations and things popular in your community. In your top five reasons to accept a job, at least three should be internal.

My initial job criteria right out of college prioritized the wrong things. I applied to all the open positions I could find because I wanted to be employed as fast as possible. I craved a high starting salary so I could show off how successful I was. And I searched for jobs with "engineer" in the title because I wanted to be respected. Now I understand that speed of employment is inconsequential in the long run. Money should have been lower on my list. And the respect of others should not have been my goal at all.

Speaking of money, moving salary lower on your list of priorities doesn't mean giving up financial stability. If you're devoted to your passion and it aligns with a need in the world, the long-term financial rewards will likely be greater. You are likely to grow and get promoted faster doing something you love than you would working a job you aren't thrilled about. Aristotle said that "Pleasure in the job puts perfection in the work." If you choose a job because of what you want rather than what other people expect of you, you'll have an easier time knocking your work duties out of the park.

After choosing a job based on criteria that prioritize *you*, work should feel quite different: You may occasionally get lost in the flow of working and forget to eat and sleep because you don't want to interrupt the fun. You'll love the work itself, not just the results of it. And you wouldn't quit even if you won a million dollars. Next, let's discuss how to find the right career that incorporates your passions.

# Discover Your Passion

The common career advice of *following your passion* doesn't quite apply when your work experiences are scarce or all alike. We discover our passions and learn what we should prioritize in a work setting by having diverse experiences.

You can search for your passions in a work environment in a number of ways. You could read job descriptions to see what sounds interesting, shadow someone to better understand the role and responsibilities, or do the work firsthand to experience it yourself. Getting hands-on experience will be the most informative—as is the case with seeking new experiences for any default setting, the most immersive experiences yield the most significant results.

One shortcut that allows for varied and in-depth exposures to different roles is working for a small business. Large organizations tend to rely on specialization, while

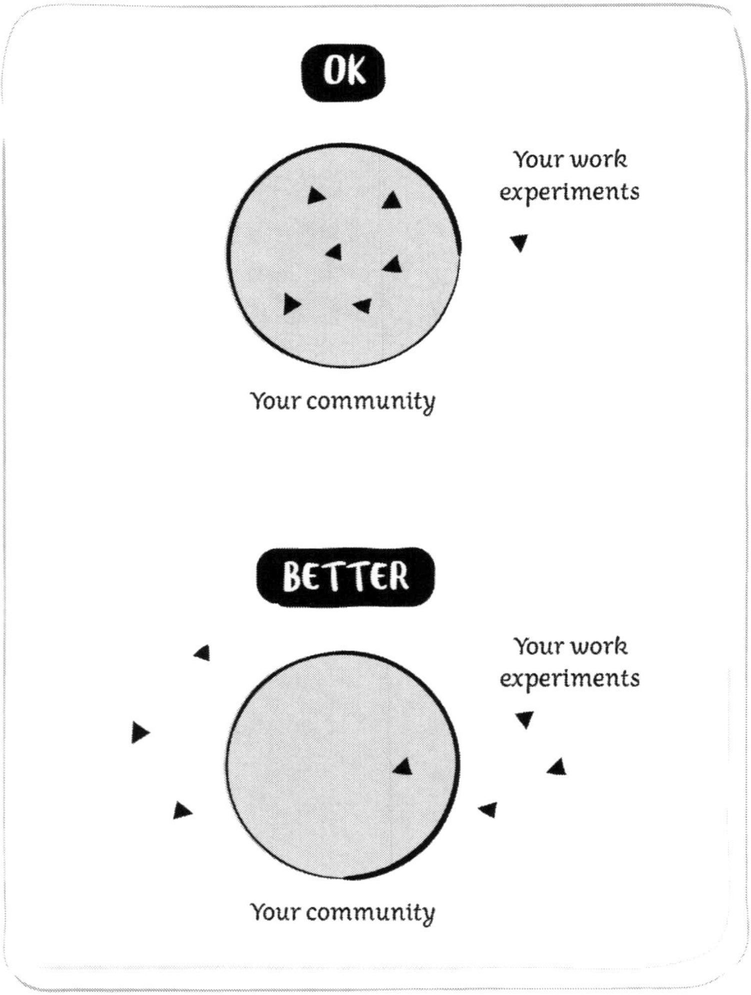
OK
Your work experiments
Your community
BETTER
Your work experiments
Your community

smaller companies often require their employees to wear multiple hats. Being a "jack of all trades" can be the perfect work environment when searching for your passion.

If you're still early in your career, emphasize learning and taking risks. One of the most common pieces of advice in investing is to allocate your money in risky assets at the beginning of your career, then gradually move your money to safer bets as you get closer to retirement. The rationale is that if you lose money when you're young, you'll have your entire life to make it up. If you lose a lot of money in a risky bet two months before you retire, however, you'll likely struggle to earn it back in time.

The same risk curve can be applied to your career decisions. Your twenties is the best time to take big risks in your career, because at the beginning, your responsibilities are limited to basic living expenses and student loan payments, and you are likely already accustomed to a frugal lifestyle thanks to your years in school.

As counterintuitive as it sounds in our culture, money *isn't* all you should aim for. Even an unpaid internship or volunteer experience incorporating your passions is better for your long-term development and success than a paid but tedious and unstimulating job. Work for minimum wage, join a start-up that may fail, start your own company, move somewhere unfamiliar, and minimize your living expenses as much as possible so you have fewer things holding you back. As you age, your list of responsibilities and expenses grows and makes it harder (but not impossible!) to make risky career decisions. You may be accountable for the security of your family, the cost of health insurance, rent, daycare expenses, and after-school activities that don't just cost money, but also infringe on your personal time. In short, take advantage of any possibility for risk now, because it will become harder as time passes.

Seeking diverse work experiences isn't easy. When you first get hands-on with tasks you haven't done, you'll be slow and inefficient, since much of it will be unfamiliar.

Fortunately, almost everything in life is a learnable skill. Any time you get negative feedback (e.g. you are labeled "a bad public speaker", "a poor leader," or "an introvert"), break the label down into individual skills (practicing your presentations more in advance, taking initiative, forming connections) that you can work on improving. An eager, flexible, and curious mindset will prevail during those transition periods of relative inexperience.

# Organize Your Data Points

If you have several work experiences under your belt, or if you've invested your time in shadowing people and trying out different types of work, you now need to turn your raw experiences into data. You do this by following the second step of adjusting a default setting: reflection.

Take inventory of what you've done. First, write down all of the positive aspects of your experiences. List the projects that came to you with surprising ease, tasks that gave you energy, and activities you want to keep learning about. Let the ideas flow without judgment or editing.

When you're done, you may notice some themes. The qualities that are repeated are the things that you'll want to repeat even more—in your full-time work or in hobbies.

# MY REFLECTION FROM MY FIRST FEW JOBS

## JOBS DONE

Quality assurance engineer
Web developer
User experience designer
Graphic designer
Office manager
Operations manager

## WHAT I LOVED

- Cross-discipline collaboration
- Solving problems, rather than executing pre-defined tasks
- Positive impact on others besides business metrics
- Opportunities to work with more experienced leaders
- Producing a design
- Respect towards employees' personal time

Now do a similar exercise with the negatives—what were the types of work you hated, the behaviors you couldn't tolerate, or the environments that weren't right for you? Benjamin Franklin said, "Those things that hurt, instruct." Knowing your frustrations will help you avoid them in the future. Or if they're systemic problems that you'd like to see fixed, you could start a project to tackle them.

The goal is to use both the positive and negative data points in your criteria for making future job decisions. Next time you're offered a job, you'll be able to interview the hiring manager with these questions: Will there be projects where you can apply your passions? Are any of your frustrations present in the new environment?

Your previous defaults were built from external inputs. Your new settings are created from your unique likes and dislikes, which will give you the confidence you need to diverge from your community's defaults to your own personal optimized defaults.

# Start a Side Project

There's one more part of your work default settings worth examining: what you do on the job. The out-of-the-box default is to follow what's spelled out in the job description, but job descriptions should be just the starting points.

Businesses stay in business as long as they provide value to their customers. This means that your job already supports people in some way, either directly on the company's front lines (especially if you work in the service or healthcare industries) or indirectly from inside an organization.

Use your passions, strengths, and frustrations to find ways to provide even more value. Improving your customers' and peers' lives in addition to your day-to-day responsibilities is a worthwhile investment. It will make you stand out and may even get you promoted faster. Here are a couple of ideas that may help you get started:

- **Apply your passions in more places.** The two takeaways from your work-related reflection—knowledge of your passions and strengths—can give you ideas about how else you can be useful to others. Can you kick-start a project to address a need you see? Could you assist with on-boarding new employees, become a mentor, or share knowledge with people outside your immediate peer group? Since your passions are activities you enjoy doing, it may not even feel like extra work to extend them to more people. Sometimes we feel like we need to ask for permission to do more than we were asked to do. Take initiative instead. Build and share a solution. Then see whether anybody else wants to join you and amplify your results.
- **Step up and solve your frustrations.** Your frustrations can be a springboard for new projects both at work and at home. If you see a process at work that bothers you, there's a good chance that it troubles others too. Propose a new template to help everybody do their jobs better in the future.

Starting new projects can be intimidating. One of the best approaches to launching something new is to take your grand idea, break it down into incremental steps, and treat each step as an experiment. If you want to change the way your company interacts with customers, pilot your idea with one team first. If your goal is to launch a new website, launch the first version with just a single key feature. Run a small test, learn from the results, and move to the next step. This approach gives each milestone more purpose, makes each step more manageable, and gets you feedback faster.

Measuring your impact is also helpful. How many hours have you spent sharing your knowledge? How many people have benefitted from the more efficient process you created? How much time have you saved yourself and your peers? Quantifying your results builds your confidence and makes it easier for other leaders to sponsor you or even join in.

# Define Success Collectively

Jony Ive once described his design team by saying: "The memory of how we work will endure beyond the products of our work." When I think back to the last few years of my projects, the most satisfying and memorable ones weren't great because of what we launched to customers, they were great because of how close our team became during the process.

In team sports, the players are invested in each other because their success is determined by their performance as a whole. It's not as easy in the workplace. Promotions and credit are usually given to individuals, not to teams. Don't be discouraged by this status quo. It only takes one person to bring a team together. And while it may take time for a team to build momentum, your chances of success in any project you tackle are multiplied when you join forces with other people and build on each other's strengths.

I've been practicing this idea of collective success for years, but there are still times I notice myself becoming too selfish in my interactions with my peers. That's when I use a trick I call the "five-year mindset" to refocus on my team: I treat my teammates as if I'll be working with them for the next five years, not just the immediate project (even when that's actually the case). By viewing your team as permanent, you approach relationships with them differently. You shift your mindset from dealing with people efficiently to investing in the team's collective expertise, taking time to understand each person's perspective, and building stronger relationships.

If you set your default to genuinely invest in partnerships at work, the memory of how your team worked together can be one of your most satisfying professional legacies.

The weight and significance of your success is based on how many people were part of it.

## Chapter Summary

- The criteria you use to accept a job will shape your entire career.
- Your criteria should prioritize your passions, strengths, and values. Money shouldn't be first on the list.
- Seek hands-on experiences to figure out what you love and what you hate.
- Optimize your career path to align with your new desires rather than your old skills. You'll pick up the necessary skills along the way.
- Don't give up on any of your passions; start side projects or hobbies to extend your impact even further.
- Invest in your team, not just in the project.

# 5

# Impact Settings

# Changing Your Work and Personal Life Defaults Isn't Enough

Having the right defaults in your personal and work life is rewarding in several ways. In your personal time, you feel more positive, you become more energized, and you have deep and fulfilling friendships. At work, you take on meaningful assignments, you pursue side projects that satisfy your passions, and you feel stable and secure.

However, stability, comfort, and the feeling that you've "made it" may nevertheless be the ultimate failure if you achieve it all without having a positive impact on other people.

There's an interview question that successful people get asked often, "What advice would you give to your

18-year-old self?" My answer would be this: *Start having a positive impact on others now. The sooner you start, the more people you'll help during your lifetime.*

No life is ever lived to its full potential if it's stable and comfortable but nothing else. Fortunately, there are many ways to have a positive impact. You can provide incremental value to thousands of people (as a business owner, a public speaker, or a content creator) or by changing the lives of a select few as a parent, volunteer, or mentor. But it will not happen by accident. The most common autopilot setting, like that of my 18-year-old self, is an internally-focused one.

To become more *externally* focused, you need to pay closer attention to the way you treat, interact with, and serve others. It's your responsibility to be deliberate about your interactions and mindful of how your work affects the rest of humanity. "Impact settings" is the last group we will analyze to ensure you're creating a legacy you're proud of.

# Avoid Indifference

> *Do good, and leave behind you a monument of virtue that the storm of time can never destroy. Write your name in kindness, love, and mercy, on the hearts of thousands you come in contact with year by year; you will never be forgotten.*
>
> \- THOMAS CHALMERS

When interacting with others, indifference is a default setting to avoid. Indifference means that we're uninterested in people who don't have something to offer us and passive about problems that don't affect us directly. When you're indifferent, your interactions are transactional and your impact on others is neutral or can even be harmful. When you care, your interactions reflect concern for the well-being of others, even when the interaction is long over. Thinking of, caring, and serving others is a better default and it allows you to impact others in a positive way.

# WHAT'S YOUR DEFAULT IN A TYPICAL MONTH?

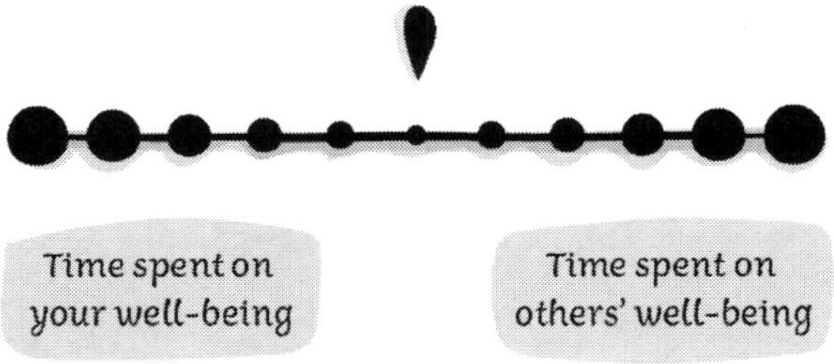


To evaluate your level of selflessness, pick a typical month and examine the amount of time you spend thinking about your happiness versus the well-being of others. Your default setting is somewhere on that spectrum. Turning the focus from yourself may seem like a big sacrifice, but I agree with what Goethe said: "He who does nothing for others does nothing for himself." Helping others means teaching, caring, loving, smiling, and being vulnerable with others, all of which will also help you grow.

Now, how exactly can you do it?

# Don't Interact Like a Business

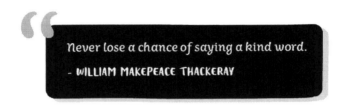

> *Never lose a chance of saying a kind word.*
>
> - WILLIAM MAKEPEACE THACKERAY

Many organizations have a principle: do things that can be replicated on a larger scale and eliminate processes that can't be uniformly applied to hundreds of customers. For example, a 45-minute phone conversation with a customer can't scale if a company has a million users. The resulting strategy is to make every customer interaction as efficient as possible or to eliminate customer contact entirely.

Too often, our mindset when interacting with others defaults to this same goal of efficiency. When we interact with others in a store, restaurant, or car repair shop, we tend to ask for what we need, finish the exchange, and move on to our next task. Companies have growth and profit goals to hit, so they treat each dialogue as a transaction. But if your goal is to have a positive impact on others, it's better to interact with empathy and attentiveness.

As you'll see in the following chapters, investing a lot of extra time into every interaction isn't necessary. All it may take is a bit of advance thought to make people feel understood, add energy to conversations, and create a stronger community. In a world where many people's default setting is indifference, it's easy to make a difference by holding a door open, or greeting people with their name, or even just smiling.

The following chapters will cover defaults during one-on-one interactions with your friends and family, and the defaults you set for others.

# Don't Just Say "Hi" to Strangers, Create New Outcomes

The following greeting is repeated millions of times every day in the U.S.:

> *Hi, how are you?*
> *I'm good, you?*
> *Good.*

Your community may have a slightly different script, but as soon as there's a default greeting in a neighborhood, we use it universally, with everybody from our baristas and teachers to our neighbors and peers. This exchange is very polite, but, like all scripts, it makes our interactions passive and impersonal. Once we say our part, we often don't even pay attention to the other person's response. Fortunately, we can choose a default that's not so superficial.

There was a professor at my college who would always smile and say "hi" to students on the way to his classroom. Once, I was sitting on a bench and saw him stop by and greet students he didn't know. What stood out to me was how the students reacted. They lifted their heads from their phones, smiled, and stood a little taller after the interaction. His actions made their day a little bit better. He did this often, almost as if he intentionally left his office early so he could interact with people he walked by and still make it to class on time. I admired his default way of interacting with others. He helped me realize that we can measure the quality of our interactions by the *outcomes* we create for other people.

What outcomes can we create for others? All humans have the same basic physical and emotional needs. We all like humor. We all wish we had more time. We all want to be treated with respect. Even without knowing somebody, you can make their day a little better by being intentional in the outcome you want to create from your interaction. Here are a few examples:

- **Plan to make people laugh.** Include a surprise twist by responding to "How are you?" in a creative way, such as "Just another day in paradise", "Getting better every minute", or "Living the dream." Say bye in a creative way, like "Make a great day!" or "Stay awesome!". Or start the conversation by telling a story about a recent amusing event (rather than only saying "hello").
- **Save people time or effort.** Hold the door for others. Stop in front of the crosswalk to let cars go through when there's a lot of traffic. Let parents with kids go in front of you in a grocery store line. Share your productivity hacks online. Don't litter.
- **Foster a sense of belonging.** Build a connection by moving from small talk to revealing a detail about yourself. Ask open-ended questions that start with "why," "when," "where," or "how." Remember personal details your teammates share with you. Look at your store clerk's name tag and call them by their name.

Get a free phone wallpaper at yourdefaultsettings.com
to remind yourself to practice different greetings.

# Help Your Loved Ones Achieve More

With strangers, you can have a positive impact by addressing their basic human needs. With your loved ones, on the other hand, you can be more proactive and the outcomes you create for them can have even greater effects. The more you know someone—your friends, spouse, or teammates—the more personalized your interactions with that person can become.

Reciprocity—helping your friend as much as they have helped you—should be the minimum. Instead, make your default to always do a little more. To start, you could celebrate their uniqueness by giving gifts that support their current life stage or surprising them with experiences tailored to their likes.

You can also help them grow. Bring them along as

you develop new skills. Introduce them to others who could advance their careers or personal life. Never say "Congrats!" alone; share specific compliments on their achievements so they gain better confidence in their strengths. Partner up to examine and change your work or personal time defaults together. For example, you can evaluate each other's work criteria or decide what new digital content you should subscribe to in order to better align with each other's goals.

To help your friends grow in areas they care about, you need to pay close attention when they share their hopes and challenges. Use questions like "What are you working toward?" and "What's missing in your life?" to stay up to date as their needs evolve. Just like you wrote down your own passions and frustrations, consider doing the same for each one of your friends. Focusing on your own personal growth is relatively easy, but helping those around you achieve more is the next level.

# Help Others Adjust Their Defaults

So far, we've covered how our communities exert their influence on us with their expectations, behaviors, and beliefs. But influence works the other way too—your routine, habits, and the way you treat others contribute to your community's identity. Philosopher Thomas Carlyle said that "Reform, like charity, must begin at home." Once we've changed ourselves, we will naturally spread that change to everything we touch, talk about, and work on.

When a new person joins your neighborhood, company, or team, they may look to you to figure out the "appropriate" way to behave, especially if you're liked by your peers or if your status or tenure implies that you can be trusted. This influence is another reason to examine and update your default settings. As soon as you improve your setting, it can be picked up by others. If you spend more time caring for others, some people may start paying it forward. If you start greeting your cashier differently, other shoppers may pay more attention to their words as well. If you're kind and thoughtful online, you may improve others' quality of dialogue as well.

If you decide to have children, your responsibility is even greater, because you automatically become a role model. Just like your parents influenced your defaults when you were growing up, you set your kids' defaults during the time you live with them and when you make decisions for your family. And just like your parents' defaults may not have been the optimal match for you, your children's settings will likely need to be different than yours.

Be sensitive to your kids' unique personalities. Let them learn to explore without your protection, without your resources, without your solutions. This is the paradox of parent-child love: sometimes, we need to distance ourselves from what we love the most. Our offspring develops stability when they're given the right roots, and they thrive proportionately to the time they're left alone to figure things out for themselves (with the security of knowing you are there for assistance if needed).

# Tiny Actions Aren't Tiny When Repeated for Years

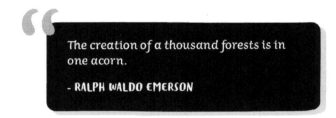

> *The creation of a thousand forests is in one acorn.*
>
> - RALPH WALDO EMERSON

At the time of this writing, the nonprofit organization *charity: water* has 73 employees. Nevertheless, the group believes that they "can end the water crisis in their lifetime." And though they are a small company and their actions may seem tiny on the day-to-day level, in their first ten years of operation, they raised 200 million dollars. Even with so much in donations, however, they know that they can't fulfill their mission overnight. Meaningful change takes time.

The outcome-focused approach of positive, proactive, and personalized one-on-one interactions won't change much immediately. It may even be uncomfortable in the short term because anytime you divert from the default way that people around you behave, it feels awkward. But change is easier when you remember the reason behind it.

The reason to update your default ways of interacting with others is a legacy of positive impact on the world. Your actions, however tiny, are building your legacy—they add up to how you'll be remembered without your money and without your possessions. There are several types of legacies: You can be remembered by the things you *create* that remain meaningful after you're gone, like Thomas Jefferson, who led the writing of the American Declaration of Independence. Or your legacy can be the things you *change* for the better, like Dr. Martin Luther King, Jr., who was instrumental in a civil rights movement. Or your impact can be immortalized by doing *selfless acts* at work and in your personal interactions, like a mother who makes consistent sacrifices for her child.

There's a common theme in all of these scenarios: the strongest legacies come from doing things differently in service of other people.

The love you send out to the world is unlike activities that give you an immediate rush, like checking tasks off your to-do list or seeing a "like" on your social media posts. The positivity that you share may not feel immediately rewarding. But keep your eye on the end game, because the positivity will carry forward. In the words of Albert Pike, a 19th-century American writer, "What we do for ourselves dies with us. What we do for others and the world remains and is immortal."

## Chapter Summary

- Impact is when you change somebody or something for the better.
- Our interactions with others are a key aspect of impact on the world. Take a positive, proactive, and personalized approach to your one-on-one interactions.
- Stay in touch with your loved ones' needs and help them achieve more.
- Others will copy your defaults, especially when you have status in your community. If you see that somebody's influences are holding them back, help them adjust their defaults.
- Meaningful change requires consistency. The legacies with the greatest impact are built when someone does things differently from those around them in service of other people.

# What's Next?

# You Deserve a Better Autopilot

You can build a life where all of the following statements are true:

- Your resume reflects your passions
- Your side projects extend your positive impact on the world
- You subscribe to entertainment that recharges you
- Your family traditions and meetings with friends create deep and generous connections
- You create new, positive outcomes for strangers
- You help your loved ones grow
- Your new default settings benefit other people in your community

In the end, the goal of adjusting all three default settings—work, personal time, and impact—is to create the change you hope to make, not just in your own life, but in the world.

You will have default settings before and after reading this book; the goal is to adjust these settings so your autopilot aligns with your goals. One of the best compliments you could get is a eulogy reflecting a life you designed for yourself and your unique goals, rather than following a safe and “appropriate” life to fit in with your community.

We first change our defaults to achieve success on our own terms, but the long-term benefit is having the energy to serve others. Author Prentice Mulford once said that goodwill to others “is the real elixir of life.” While life is finite, your impact is not.

# WHICH ONE WILL BE YOU?

# Three Things That Can Help You Commit

At its core, this book is dedicated to motivating you to change. If you've ever tried a new diet, a new exercise program, or a new habit from a book, you know that it's hard to stick with anything new. The hardest part is the beginning. Unfortunately, there isn't just one beginning. Every day is a new start—with new distractions and responsibilities outside the "change" that your past self signed up for. By default, we return to our previous, comfortable routine or we keep waiting for the right time to begin.

However, there are three tactics that can be helpful in jump-starting a change in your life:

## Have a Strong "Why"

Articulate your "why" for changing. Your *why* is a unique type of motivation. It's motivation tied to something that's not on the horizon, but in the far future, such as the hope of leaving a positive legacy.

A strong "why" is unlikely to change. It will be the north star that can help you shift to a different gear and follow up on a change that you promised you would make. If you want to change, figure out your long-term why and revisit it when you're tempted to procrastinate.

# NEW IDEAS ARE SMALL SEEDS

## Find What Throws You Off

The second tactic is to change something in your environment that can throw you off your old routine. This could be:

1. Changing your surroundings, such as switching from your desk to a comfortable recliner. Or moving to a darker room. Or a lighter room. Or visiting a place where others are productive, such as a library or a coffee shop.
2. Listening to your favorite music that transports you to a different state of mind. It could be the lyrics of one song that you play on repeat (for me, this is Andy Grammer's song "Masterpiece"), or a special playlist reserved for the time you work on your new goals.
3. Triggering a change in body chemistry, by drinking a caffeinated drink, taking a cold shower, or getting your heart pumping with a quick exercise session that can jolt you out of procrastination. A set of ten push-ups is my go-to exercise that stops my dilly-dallying.

## Set up Reminders

The third tactic that can help you make a lasting change is to set up reminders. Our memory has a limited capacity. We come across so many good ideas, but even when the best ones fascinate us, they often get replaced by things we encounter in our daily routine, by a work deadline, or by a negative news cycle.

While you'll never be able to completely eliminate the distractions, you can try placing visual reminders in your physical and digital world to remind yourself of your "why" and of the new ideas you're trying to implement. I'm a big fan of integrating reminders into what's already around you: a poster on your bathroom door, a sticker on your laptop, a wallpaper on your smartphone, or a wristband on your...wrist. Go to **yourdefaultsettings.com** to get free products that will act as your reminders—they may help you get started on your new journey.

No single tactic will be your solution. Be on the hunt for the combination of environmental tweaks and reminders that will help you change. Get started now—it may be later than you think.

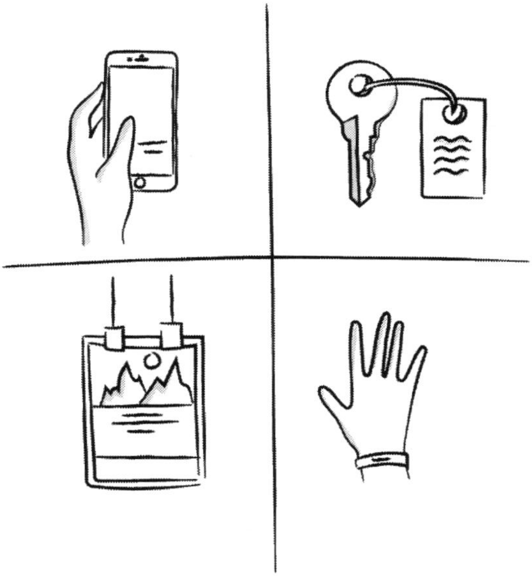

Place physical reminders in your environment to better retain new ideas.

Get free resources at yourdefaultsettings.com

# How to Save Time, Save Money, and Be Healthier

This book covered groups of default settings in three areas of your life: work, personal time, and impact, but the framework of examining and adjusting your defaults applies elsewhere, too. There are defaults you can examine that could increase your effectiveness in any area. For example, in simple everyday tasks—perhaps there's a way you could brush your teeth to make them whiter and healthier, or a faster way to tie your shoes, or a route to work that would make your car use less gas. This also applies to products and services in your life: maybe your phone could be optimized to load faster or your bank account could be tweaked to save you money.

To get occasional emails with practical tips on adjusting your defaults in all areas of your life, go to **yourdefaultsettings.com/newsletter**

Discuss default settings in your life and connect with others who are also trying to change their defaults at **yourdefaultsettings.com/community**

Share the progress of your journey with a hashtag **#yourdefaultsettings**

# Thank You

**To my wife,** Laura, for her hard questions, continuous support, and letting me work on this project during mornings, evenings, weekends, and vacation days for nearly three years.

• • •

**To my editors**, Ameesha Green, Stephanie Carbajal, and Blair Thornburgh for helping me with...well, all aspects of book writing. Your expertise was invaluable.

• • •

**To my design mentors**, Michael Zaletel, Lisa Quirin, Niki Dare, Jerrod Larson, Danielle Teska, David Cole, and Kris Bell, for guiding and challenging me to always do better. Your high standards have made me a more disciplined thinker.

**To my soccer coaches,** Janusz Czerniewicz, David Wilson, John Gray, and Chris Scotti, for your advice on and off the field in some of the most formative years of my life.

• • •

**To my teachers**, Leonard Ornstein, Penny Ann Dolin, and Thomas Schildgen, for seeing more potential in me than I ever felt I had.

• • •

**To my fellow authors and artists**, Simon Sinek, Seth Godin, Steven Pressfield, William Zinsser, Austin Kleon, Zig Ziglar, and Napoleon Hill, whose words and work have inspired me to keep going no matter what, and to Andy Grammer and Kaleo, for creating amazing music that I listened to on loop during countless hours of writing and rewriting this book.

# About the Author

Rad Wendzich is an award-winning designer with over a decade of experience designing default settings in technology. Through his blog, products, and communities he's created, he helps people break away from the expectations and norms that limit their growth. He lives with his family in Seattle, Washington, and online at radwendzich.com.

Made in the USA
Middletown, DE
29 January 2020

83879748R00086